SURVIVAL CHALLENGE

EMERGENCY!

Could YOU deal with disaster in the world's wildest places?

STEPHANIE TURNBULL

A⁺
Smart Apple Media

Published by Smart Apple Media,
an imprint of Black Rabbit Books
P.O. Box 3263, Mankato, Minnesota, 56002
www.blackrabbitbooks.com

Designed and illustrated by Guy Callaby
Edited by Mary-Jane Wilkins

Cataloging-in-Publication Data is available from the Library of Congress

ISBN 978-1-62588-214-1

Photo acknowledgements
t = top; c = center; b = bottom; r = right; l = left
folio image Olga Ryabtsova/Thinkstock; 2l Steve Collender, b PaulShlykov;
3 Mike Buchheit; 4 Ammit Jack/all Shutterstock; b Ciaran Griffin;
    5tl Stockbyte/both Thinkstock, tr szpeti/Shutterstock, b Ljupco/Thinkstock;
      6 ZStoimenov/Shutterstock; 7 Sergey Mostovoy; 8t Ramonespelt/both
        Thinkstock, b Darren J. Bradley/Shutterstock; 10t seaskylab/Thinkstock,
         l Eric Isselee; 11t Maria Dryfhout/both Shutterstock, r Henrik_L/Thinkstock;
         12 Toa55; 13 holbox; 14 My Good Images; 16t andreiuc88/all Shutterstock,
          b © Alvin Burrows; 17 Sean Martin; 18t Kevin Fourie/all Thinkstock, l Guy J.
          Sagi; 19 Microstock Man/Shutterstock; 20t © Daniel Cardiff/Thinkstock,
          b RHIMAGE; 23 Ron Kacmarcik
          Cover t Sashkin/Shutterstock, b Jupiterimages/Thinkstock

Printed in China

DAD0056
032014
9 8 7 6 5 4 3 2 1

CONTENTS

TAKE THE CHALLENGE

Imagine you're an intrepid explorer trekking across crumbling clifftops, scorching deserts, steamy jungle swamps or windswept Arctic wastes.

Something doesn't feel right. What's that noise? The rumble of approaching thunder, the low growl of an unseen creature or the crackle of distant flames? And is it your imagination, or is the ground moving—or sinking—below your feet?

Your heart pounds as the horrible truth hits you. You're alone and in BIG trouble.

Your challenge is to avoid disaster— fast. Can you do it?

Disaster can strike in many ways
in the wild. Rock falls, lightning strikes
and blizzards can all be deadly.
Do you have the nerve to face an
emergency and the skills to escape it?

KEEP CALM

First things first: don't panic. To survive a wilderness emergency you need to keep a clear head. Stop and think before doing anything—otherwise you may make a bad situation worse.

BE PREPARED

Good planning can help you avoid many dangerous situations. If you're smart, you'll have worked out a route that avoids hazards such as cliffs or swamps—or at least have looked at alternative paths in case you suddenly need to change course.

REAL LIFE SURVIVAL

A hiker named Mary O'Brien got lost in the snowy Washington mountains without a map or any survival gear. She spent five terrifying days wandering alone in the wilderness. Eventually she found a river and was spotted by people in a boat.

Never set out without a good map to help you find your way or plan a route.

TAKE THE RIGHT GEAR

Let's hope you remembered to pack a good survival kit. This should contain essential items such as a map, compass, matches, knife, rope, safety pins, blanket and first-aid box.

↻ *Make sure your survival kit isn't too heavy to carry comfortably.*

KNOW FIRST AID

A first-aid kit may not be much use in a serious disaster, but it can help treat minor wounds.

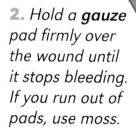

1. *Remove any dirt from the wound, then clean it with cotton wool and clean water. Dab dry with a clean cloth.*

2. Hold a **gauze** pad firmly over the wound until it stops bleeding. If you run out of pads, use moss.

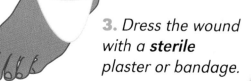

3. *Dress the wound with a **sterile** plaster or bandage.*

Climbing mountains or scrambling over rocks can be dangerous. You may lose your footing and slip, or a rock fall could crush you. So watch out!

THINK FIRST

Before you begin to climb, check how far you would fall if you slipped. Would you just slither a short way down a gentle slope? Start climbing carefully. Could you plummet into an **abyss**? Turn back or find another route.

↻ *Remember to wear sturdy footwear if you'll be crossing tough, rocky terrain.*

↻ *Use your head—don't seek shelter under rocks that might fall on you!*

ROCK FALLS

In steep valleys, don't ignore loose, crumbly paths or small falls of stones —these could lead to huge rock falls. If rocks do fall, get away fast, and don't be tempted to return. There could be more to come.

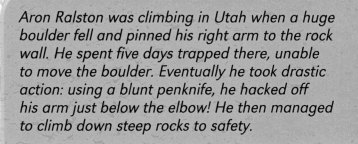

AVALANCHE!

Avalanches are masses of snow that slide rapidly down mountainsides, often when the temperature rises and snow melts. Many places likely to have avalanches are signposted, so pay attention to these warnings.

Some avalanches are so huge that rocks and trees are dragged along with them.

9

AVOID ANIMALS

Disturbing a wild animal is not a good move—and it could be your last. Beasts such as bears, crocodiles and cougars can kill. But they only attack if they feel threatened, so look out for animal homes and stay away!

BE BEAR AWARE

Here's what NOT to do in bear territory. These tips could save your life.

🐻 Don't go crashing through undergrowth. Stick to paths and camp in open areas.

🐻 Don't leave food or anything smelly uncovered. Store it in sealed bags.

🐻 Don't run away from a bear. If it's far away, back off slowly. If it's close to your camp, make lots of noise, such as shouting and banging pans, to scare it off.

🐻 Don't climb a tree. Grizzly bears are good climbers, so they'll be right behind you.

⮑ *Hang sealed food bags up high, like this, so bears can't reach them.*

Nell and Jim Hamm were hiking in California when a cougar pounced on Jim and grabbed his head in its jaws. Nell whacked the animal with a log to make it let go, then screamed to scare it away. Luckily, this worked. The cougar retreated and Nell and Jim hurried to safety.

REAL LIFE SURVIVAL

↶ *A snake rearing up ready to strike is not something you want to see!*

⮑ *This mosquito is full of blood after feasting on a tasty human.*

SNAKE BITES

All snakes can bite, but it's the venomous ones you need to worry about—they have two fangs that leave large, painful puncture marks in skin. Some snake bites are deadly, so get help as quickly as possible (see pages 20-21). Wash the area with soap and water, but never cut the skin to try to get rid of the venom. It won't work!

SMALL BUT DEADLY

Sometimes the deadliest animals are the ones you don't see, such as mosquitoes, which can transmit **malaria**, and ticks, which can pass on **Lyme disease**. Use insect repellent, wear long sleeves and pants and sleep under mosquito nets if you can.

STAY ON SOLID GROUND

If you're hiking along river banks, wading through marshes or trudging over soggy sand, the ground may not be stable. Follow these tips to avoid getting a nasty sinking feeling...

USE YOUR HEAD

Try to avoid wet ground. Is there another way you can go? It may take longer, but it beats getting stuck in mud! If you have to battle through a bog, stick to areas with lots of vegetation so you have something to grab if you lose your footing.

Steamy tropical forests like this are full of squishy bugs and slimy logs to slip on.

WATCH FOR ROOTS

Crossing a swamp is hard work. The water can be deep and clogged with tangled, slippery roots. It's better to go by boat, though you still risk getting lost in a maze of waterways. Be sure to take a map.

⊃ *The marshy Everglades of Florida contain alligators, too.*

DON'T STRUGGLE

Quicksand is oozing, wet sand that can suck you in with surprising force. If this happens, don't struggle or you'll sink deeper. Lie flat on your back or stomach to spread your weight. Slowly wriggle, snake-like, toward drier land.

Robbie Tesar was hiking in Utah when he stepped on a sandy riverbank and was sucked up to his waist into quicksand. The heavy mud acted like concrete, holding him so tightly he couldn't move his legs. He was stuck for 13 hours before a rescue team on rafts managed to pull him out.

REAL LIFE SURVIVAL

13

BE WATER-WISE

Finding a river in the wilderness may save your life, offering you drinking water and a route back to civilization. But beware—water can be dangerous, too.

FLOOD WARNING

Never camp on low land near water. Heavy rain can make rivers burst their banks and flood nearby areas with alarming speed. In deserts, sudden rain creates rivers that gush through narrow **gorges**, sweeping away everything in their path—including you.

CROSS WITH CAUTION

Wading through rivers is a bad idea, as the **current** may be stronger than you realize. Cross at a bridge, even if it means going out of your way to find one. If you really must wade, here's how.

1. Find a wide section of river where the water is shallower and the current less fierce. Don't use rocks as stepping stones; they may be slippery.

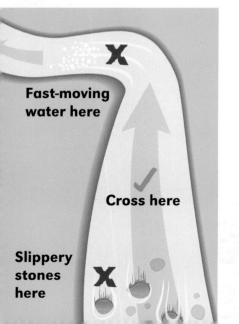

Fast-moving water here

X

✓ Cross here

Slippery stones here

X

2. Take off your shoes to keep them dry, then step cautiously into the water. If it's higher than your knees, turn back. Drag your feet—don't lift them—to avoid losing your balance. Try using a pole for support.

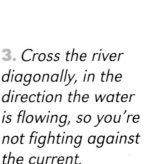

3. Cross the river diagonally, in the direction the water is flowing, so you're not fighting against the current.

WATCH THE WEATHER

Wild weather can cause all kinds of emergencies. Fog, heavy snow or rain can make you lose your way—or your footing—and severe storms can kill you on the spot. But don't despair when you see dark clouds approaching. Act fast!

STOP AND SHELTER

In a sudden blizzard or sandstorm, find shelter as quickly as possible. Wait until the weather improves, then use your map and compass to check you're still on course.

➲ *Need help with navigation? Look for another book in this series, **Survival Challenge: Lost!***

BRACE YOURSELF

Tornadoes are huge, swirling columns of wind that race along at speeds of more than 480 km/h (300 mph), ripping up trees and flinging debris in the air. If you're unlucky enough to be in a tornado's path, crouch on low ground, away from large objects that could topple onto you.

Brace yourself like this and hope for the best.

Mauro Prosperi was running in a grueling long-distance race across the Sahara Desert when a sandstorm blew up. Confused and blinded by sand, he got completely lost and spent nine terrifying days alone in the desert before being rescued.

REAL LIFE SURVIVAL

A small cave may look safe, but lightning can flow through rock, jump a gap and strike you!

GO LOW

Lightning strikes the highest point, so never shelter under trees in a storm. Get down from hills or high ridges and crouch low. Lightning can travel through the ground, so sit on your backpack.

BEWARE OF FIRE

Forest fires are one of nature's biggest dangers. In dry, windy weather, fires spread at incredible speed, racing through undergrowth and engulfing trees in a wall of flame. Don't think you're safe because a fire is miles away—move NOW.

🎧 Animals sense and react to fire before you see it.

GO AROUND

You can't outrun a forest fire. Instead, try to go around it, heading away from the direction the wind is blowing. Don't go uphill—fire spreads upward quickly as heat rises. Aim for clear, open areas of low ground.

Don't hide in a cave; it could heat up like an oven. And never jump into a pool of water! The water could become boiling hot.

MAKE A BURROW

If there's no chance of escape, bury yourself in dry ground and hope the fire will pass over you. It's a risk: the ground will heat up, and the fire may burn so much **oxygen** that you can't breathe. So let's hope you never have to try this!

⟳ *The landscape after a forest fire can look completely different.*

⋂ *Don't start a wildfire yourself! Rake over the* ***embers*** *of campfires and pour water on them.*

In 1910, Idaho forest ranger Ed Pulaski saved 40 members of his team when a huge fire they were fighting broke out of control. Thinking fast, he led the men to an abandoned mine where they sheltered safely. Pulaski later designed an ax which would clear undergrowth and help stop fires from spreading.

REAL LIFE SURVIVAL

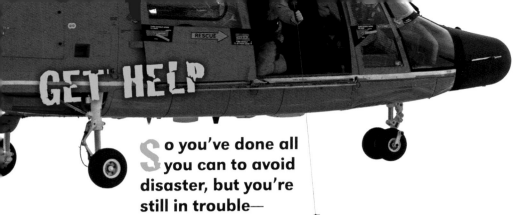

So you've done all you can to avoid disaster, but you're still in trouble—perhaps injured, ill or hopelessly lost. Time to get expert help!

↶ *Mountain rescue teams often lift stranded climbers to safety by helicopter.*

BE SEEN

If you were smart enough to pack a **signal flare**, use it! If not, attract the attention of aircraft by making signs on high, open ground with sticks, rocks or bright clothing.

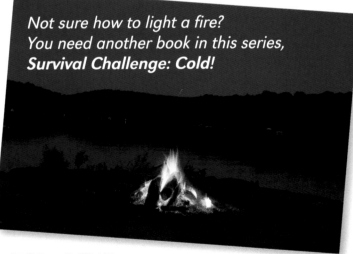

Not sure how to light a fire? You need another book in this series, Survival Challenge: Cold!

A torch flashing on and off may be seen from the ground or air.

LIGHT A FIRE

At night, a campfire burning in an open space might be spotted. But put it out carefully afterwards so it doesn't spread and cause more problems! If possible, light three fires in a triangle. This is an international signal for help.

In daylight, make a log frame and light a fire inside.

Pile on **evergreen** branches to produce lots of smoke that will be seen for miles.

SIGNAL TO AIRCRAFT

If a rescue helicopter spots you, stand at a safe distance from where it will land and communicate with the pilot using these hand signals.

Hold your arms straight up to tell the pilot you want to be picked up.

Move your arms slowly up and down to tell the pilot it's safe to descend.

GLOSSARY

abyss
A very deep gorge or crack in the ground.

current
A mass of water flowing in one definite direction.

ember
A glowing, hot fragment of wood or other fuel, left when a fire has burned down.

evergreen
A tree or plant that keeps its leaves all through the year. Pine, fir and spruce trees are all evergreens.

gauze
A type of fine cotton cloth used for bandages and other first-aid dressings.

gorge
A deep valley between cliffs, sometimes called a canyon.

Lyme disease
A disease that causes a rash, fever and aches. If left untreated, it can seriously damage the heart, brain, nerves, joints and eyes.

malaria
A disease passed on through mosquito bites. It can cause chills and fever and may be fatal. If you're visiting a place where malaria is common, take anti-malaria drugs before you go.

oxygen
An invisible gas in the air around us. We need oxygen to breathe, and fires use it to burn.

signal flare
A device that produces a blaze of light, like a firework without the bang.

sterile
Completely clean and free from bacteria.

22

www.comingbackalive.com
How to deal with all kinds of emergencies, including avalanches, hurricanes, wild animals and many more.

www.backpacker.com/survival
Hints and tips for packing survival gear and surviving disaster in the wilderness.

www.thesurvivalexpert.co.uk/SurvivalSituationsCategory.html
Advice on every worst-case scenario you can imagine!

INDEX